Welcome to Estonia

Where the continuous curving line of the eastern Baltic coast suddenly breaks to give way to major indentations, a chunk of land juts out into the sea, with two large and numerous small islands lying immediately west of it. That land, squeezed between the Gulf of Riga in the south and the Gulf of Finland in the north, is Estonia.

Compared with countries such as Belgium, the Netherlands and Denmark, Estonia, with its 45,215 square kilometres of territory, is not so small at all. But the country has only about 1.5 million inhabitants, and if the population density were as high as in Singapore, they would only take up a corner of one of its islands. One third of the population lives in Tallinn, leaving the rest of the country rather sparsely inhabited.

To make up for it, Estonia boasts of vast areas of almost virgin nature, from deserted sandy beaches lined with pine woods to bogs and wetlands, which have nearly disappeared from the rest of Europe, and rolling uplands in the south-east of the country. The highest elevation in Estonia is Suur-Munamägi, 318 metres above sea level. This is quite a lot for Estonia, particularly considering the fact that the western, central and northern parts of the country are nearly flat. In the north, the plains end in abrupt limestone cliffs which drop down to the sea below.

The Lahemaa National Park in north central Estonia is always worth a visit. Besides scenic coastal views, if offers beautiful walks through pine woods and peat bogs with open pools, old fishing villages, such as **Käsmu** and **Altja**, as well as nicely restored manor halls at **Palmse**, **Sagadi** and **Vihula**, all set in extensive parks. These manorial complexes, as well as many other throughout the country, are witnesses of Estonia's Baltic-German past.

The islands constitute a world by themselves. The biggest of the roughly 1,500 islands are **Saaremaa** and **Hiiumaa**, which have already been discovered by many foreign guests. But this does not mean there are no deserted beaches and juniper groves left over for you – the islands are large enough for this! A trip to some of thesmaller islands such as **Kihnu** or **Ruhnu** will award you with a real exotic setting in the blue, and sometimes, grey, expanse of the Baltic.

A favourite with summer visitors is the green seaside resort of **Pärnu** on Estonia's western coast. In summer, the town even takes over as the country's summer capital. But if you are more interested in culture and history, you should schedule a trip to **Tartu**, the site of one of the oldest universities in northern Europe and the cradle of Estonian national culture.

It shouldn't be a serious problem to see most of the country during your visit, because it is really small in size. From one end of Estonia to another and back is a convenient day's drive. This is the advantage of a small country, and the Estonians' generally good linguistic skills help make such a trip a success.

As the Estonians' own language is only spoken by about one million people, command of foreign languages, at least on a basic level, becomes a must. English and Russian are understood nearly everywhere, and many people can also express themselves in German, Finnish or Swedish. But you may run into difficulties when asking directions in outlying parts of the country, so it would be wise to rely on a good map.

The Estonian language belongs to the Finno-Ugric family and is mutually comprehensible, to a degree, only with Finnish. It is not at all related to the languages of any of the other neighbouring peoples – that of the Russians, who speak a Slavic language, or Latvian and Lithuanian which form the Baltic group. To understand these languages, Estonians first

have to learn them as foreign tongues. But where one wants to find a common language, this is never a problem.

The Estonians love their land, their language and their culture, as they certainly do their stern Nordic nature. It is at its best in June, when the summer is still young and the lilacs blossom, spreading their intoxicating smell all around, and making young hearts sing.

June, particularly toward the end of the month, is also the time of short, light nights when the sun only drops below the horizon for a few hours. St. John's Eve, 23 June, at about the summer solstice is the biggest summer festival to mark the shortest night of the year. It is celebrated by lighting bonfires and merrymaking around them, and young people leave the fireside in pairs to go looking for the fortune-bringing fern flower, believed to blossom on that single night during the year.... According to an Estonian legend, two lovers, Twilight and Dawn, fleetingly meet that night thanks to its brevity and exchange a kiss. It is a night to become poetic, or then to grumble, why don't they put out the light!

Welcome in Tallinn

Tallinn, capital of the Republic of Estonia, has about 434,000 inhabitants of whom about half are Estonian-speaking.

Tallinn is not just the capital and the biggest city of the country, but also the most important port and transport terminal as well as Estonia's cultural metropolis. It has numerous theatres, concert halls and museums, of which perhaps the most outstanding are the Estonia Opera and Ballet Theatre and concert hall, and the Estonian Art Museum. Naturally, Tallinn has much more to offer in the way of cultural entertainment, and when you take a tour in the Old Town you will find a gallery, an antiques shop, a museum or an exhibition in nearly every one of its winding streets and lanes. For refreshments there are numerous cellar bars, cosy restaurants and, in summer, also street cafes to offer you a cup of coffee, a mug of beer or something more substantial. In summer you may get the opportunity of attending an open-air concert or a theatrical performance, so ask your hotel desk for information. But first of all, a walk through the Old City is an exciting tour about the history of the town and the whole of Estonia.

The Citadel on a Limestone Bank

Tallinn rises from the sea like a fairy-tale city. The citadel of **Toompea** is easily recognised in its skyline, thanks to its elevated position above the rest of the historical centre, or All-linn, the Lower Town. The Estonian national epic Kalevipoeg, a narrative heroic poem by Friedrich Reinhold

Kreutzwald (1803-1882), recounts in one of its episodes how Toompea was born. When Kalev, the old king, died, his widow Linda decided to heap a mound of stones on his grave. Carrying the stones from all around in her apron, her apron-string snapped, the stone dropped from her lap and she sat down on it and wept. A lake was born of the tears. Kalev's grave mound is

today identified as Toompea and the pool made by Linda's tears as **Lake Ülemiste**, the expanse of water just opposite Tallinn's airport. The lake even has a large rock near its water line, known as **Linda's Rock.** There is a monument to Kalev's mourning widow, by the noteworthy sculptor August Weizenberg (1837-1921), near the **Pikk Hermann** tower on Toompea. According to a legend everyone in Tallinn can tell you, Lake Ülemiste is the abode of a grey old man who comes out on dark autumn nights to ask if the city is finally completed. If the answer should be yes, the old man goes back and floods the city with all the people in it. But the people need not fear, because building never ceases in the city.

Kolyvan, Lyndanise, Reval or Tallinn?

"A good child has many names," goes an Estonian proverb. Obviously, Tallinners love their town very much, because it has had a number of names during its history. A somewhat less light-hearted explanation is that each ruler called the city by a different name. The oldest recorded name of the city is Kolyvan, probably a derivation from the name Kalev. Kolyvan is the name by which Tallinn was first indicated on a world map by the Arab geographer al-Idrisi in **1154**. This is also the first written mention of the city in historical records and is regarded as the year of the city's foundation. Another

4

old name, Lyndanise, is found in the 13th century Chronicle of Henricus de Lettis. The Germans, who in one form or another ruled over Estonia for seven centuries, called the place **Reval**, after the name of the old Estonian county of Rävala.

During the period of Russian imperial rule, the German name Reval was modified to **Revel**. These are all names by which the town was known to its rulers. For the Estonians themselves the city came to be called **Tallinn**. This is believed to be a derivation from Taani linn, Estonian for Danish castle, after the first foreign conquerors of the place in the 13th century. In the course of time, Taani linn has gradually been shortened to Tallinn - the present official name of the city.

Location of the City

Why was the 11th century Estonian hill fort built at the place where Tallinn lies now? The answer is not difficult to see. A wide protected bay with two outlying islands, **Aegna** and **Naissaar**, serving as landmarks to navigators crossing the Gulf of Finland at its narrowest place on a busy east-west sea route served as a good precondition to the rise of a harbour. The oldest traces of settlement in Tallinn are from the area opposite the Olümpia Hotel where it was established on the banks of the River Härjapea (Oxhead), now closed into underground pipes. As late as the early 2nd millennium A.D. it still flew into the bay in the area between the present Kaubamaja department store and the Olümpia Hotel, but as the land continued to rise the harbour moved from its mouth to where it is now.

The steep limestone rock of Toompea, with a flat surface of 8 hectares rising high above the surrounding coastal lowland,

must have been a splendid location for a hill fort to offer protection to the people in case of danger. It is therefore no wonder that already in the 12th century news of the port had reached as far as Sicily where al-Idrisi worked in King Roger's court. At least six trade routes led from the interior of the land into the harbour, which was visited also by foreign ships. The trade routes met at the market place, today's **Raekoja plats, Town Hall Square**, and from there busy streets (the present Pikk and Vene Streets) led into the harbour, while the steep Pikk jalg served as a way up to Toompea. Thanks to the surviving original street network the structure of the Old Town can be easily recognised even today. The city was built up with three aspects in mind - as a fortress, a port and a marketplace. Merchants' houses with warehouses for the storage of goods were built along the streets leading from the port to the market place, and all manner of artisans set up shop near the market. In the 14th and the 15th centuries guild houses were built in the main street and a town hall in the market place. Thus the so-called **all-linn, Lower Town**, gradually sprang up at Toompea's foot.

Close to the port, boatmen, pilots, fishermen and fishmongers built their houses quite near the port in **Kalamaja**, one of Tallinn's oldest suburbs outside the town wall, while another old suburb was situated near the present **St. John's almshouse** (Jaani seek) and the Olümpia Hotel on the banks of the Härjapea River. Idrisi the map-maker wrote about Tallinn in the 12th century: "The people leave the town in winter and return there in spring". It is quite possible that people lived in the original wooden fortress on Toompea only in the summer. The wooden structure was replaced by a stone one only after the foreign conquest in the early 13th century. As evidence of those times, the castle's corner towers retain their old German names, as do the towers of the wall around the Lower Town.

A Gift from Heaven

In 1193 Pope Clement III ordered that Crusades be organised not only against the non-Christians in the Holy Land but also against the pagans in Northern Europe. In 1219 King Waldemar II of Denmark landed with his fleet at Tallinn. A bloody battle broke out, which the Danes saw they were losing. Then bishop Andrew looked up into the heaven and there a miracle occurred - the gates of Heavens opened and a red flag with a white cross on it dropped down from the skies into the bishop's hands. Taking this for a sign of God, the Danes found new courage and won the battle. So goes a legend about how the Danes got their national flag, the **Danebrog,** in a battle with the Estonians. The Danes chased the Estonians from Toompea and built their own stone fortress to replace the Estonians' wooden stronghold. But ten years later they had to temporarily relinquish their rule over North Estonia to the German order of Sword Brethren, who had been driving into the country from the south, converting the pagan Estonians to Christianity by fire and sword. The Knights, together with the bishops, established a permanent rule over all Estonia only in 1346, when Denmark sold its possessions in Estonia to the Sword Brethern's successor, the Teutonic Knights.

Tallinn in the Hanseatic League

When the Knights of the Sword briefly ruled over Tallinn in the 1220s, they decided to turn the place into a German city and invited 200 German merchants from Visby in Gotland to settle in Tallinn. This dictated a German frame of mind in Tallinn even in the days of Danish rule, and in 1284 the town became a member in the **Hanseatic League** of German trading towns which paved the way to its prosperity throughout the Middle Ages. From the beginning of the 13th century onwards the town actually consisted of two distinct parts, each with its own interests and laws. The Upper Town on Toompea was the seat of the mainly German-born landed gentry, and the Lower Town at Toompea's foot a free city of merchants and craftsmen. As there were continuous arguments between the two communities, a wall was built in the 14th century to separate

the two parts of the town. Even the doors and gates in the wall were locked and bolted for the night. This separation of the town was only abolished at the end of the 19th century. Fortunately, the Old Town of Tallinn has managed to retain its medieval appearance relatively unchanged in its complexity. Even more than in extant individual buildings, the Old Town's value lies in the integrity of its medieval structure. This is also the ground why in 1997 the Old Town of Tallinn was entered into the **UNESCO World Heritage List.** The Old Town still has its medieval street network with Hanseatic period guild and citizens' houses, as well as its old town wall with fortification towers from the 14th-16th centuries. In the 13th and the 14th centuries the Lower Town with its low wooden houses and vegetable gardens must have looked like a large village. But thanks to the growing wealth of the population on the one hand and compelled by the frequent fires one the other hand bigger and prettier houses were gradually built. The streets were cobbled and partly covered with stone slabs. In 1360 the municipal government ordered that each house owner sweep the front of his house every Saturday to prevent the people from soiling their clothes as they went to church on Sunday. On weekdays such work was done by the town's executioner, but he only carted away the worst rubbish. In the 15th century Tallinn grew into an important trading town. All kind of goods arrived here from the West – salt, fabrics, weapons, wines, herrings in transit to Russia, above all the Hanseatic trading station in Novgorod. Russian goods, such as bear hides, leather, honey, fish, linen, hemp and tar was shipped back through Tallinn to the west. One of the most important trade articles was salt. It was even said that Tallinn was built on salt. In the 16th century Tallinn with its 7,000-8,000 inhabitants was among the biggest cities in northern Europe. The coats of arms of four Hanseatic towns, Bruges, Novgorod, London and Bergen, decorate the front of the Brotherhood of the Blackheads in Pikk Street, and also the coat of arms of Tallinn on a shipping company bench in Lübeck is proof of a prospering past and Tallinn's relations with the other trading towns of the Hanseatic League. But no glitter lasts forever. The power of the Hansa was broken, trade with salt started to decline and Tallinn gradually lost its economic importance. The times of Hanseatic trade were over.

Through the Livonian War to the "Good Old Swedish Time"

In 1558 Russia under Ivan the Terrible started a devastating war against Old Livonia (lands held by the Livonian Order north of the Daugava River). The Russians at first made considerable headway, and some of their troops even appeared outside Tallinn's walls in the very first year of the war. Because of Old Livonia's weakness as a state structure, both the corporation of nobility on Toompea and the Town Council of Tallinn decided to take an oath of allegiance to King Erik XIV of Sweden early on in the war, in summer 1561. By that time the island of Saaremaa had passed under Danish rule and Poland established its rule over southern Estonia. All these powers, as well as Russia, rushed to seize a bigger piece of present-day Estonia. For the country, this meant indescribable hardship. Tallinn was besieged twice by Russian armies, in 1570–71 and 1577. At the same time, there were outbreaks of epidemics in the besieged city. The longest of the sieges lasted nearly thirty weeks, but the town's fortifications were strong, provisions were brought in from the sea and the town never surrendered.

Hostilities lasted until 1583 and under peace treaties which Russia signed with Poland and Sweden in 1582 and 1583, Estonia remained divided between Sweden, Denmark and Poland. But peace didn't last long. Only a few years later fighting was resumed between Russia, Sweden, Poland and Denmark, bringing more epidemics and hunger. By 1629, Sweden managed to establish control over the whole of present-day

Estonia. An epidemic broke out in 1603, a fire destroyed nearly all houses in Tallinn's Toompea area, and 1695–97 were the years of great hunger. And yet this period in Estonian history is known as the "good old Swedish time". Obviously the times before and also after must have been still worse. Although Tallinn's rights were restricted during the Swedish period, it must also be admitted that a foundation was laid to the Estonian school system during the rule of King Gustavus II Adolphus when secondary schools, "gymnasiums" were opened in Tartu and Tallinn. The most important step, however, was the founding of a university in Tartu in 1632.

A teacher's seminar was founded and schools for the children of the peasantry were opened in various parts of the country. For the middle of the 17th century, these were progressive developments. If for example in Russia eradication of illiteracy only started after 1917, then Estonia's adult population was 98 percent literate as early as 1886.

Under the Rule of the Double-headed Eagle

Under the Swedish rule, peasants were granted the right to own property as well as the right to sue their lords. The rights of the nobility, however, were cut back considerably. Therefore it was no wonder that with their wings cropped by Sweden, the nobility were rather well disposed towards Russia when it launched the Northern War in 1700 under Peter I. The reason was the same Ivan IV had had in the 16th century - to carve an opening on to the Baltic Sea. Russian troops invaded Estonia once again. In Tallinn, the hostile attacks and renewed outbreaks of epidemics forced the Swedish garrison, the nobility corporation and the citizens to surrender to the Russians after a six-week siege in 1710. This satisfied the Russian ruler, but did not put an end to the plague. Of the earlier 9,801 inhabitants only 1,962 souls remained alive in the town. After the Northern War ended, Russian General Sheremetyev could report: "From Narva to Riga one cannot hear a dog barking or a rooster crowing." The land had really had to suffer enormous hardship. Under the peace treaty signed between Russia and Sweden in Uusikaupunki, Finland, the Baltic lands were assigned to Russia. Local authority, however, remained in the hands of the Baltic-German nobility who had vowed allegiance to the Czar. The Baltic barons achieved confirmation of all their former rights, including those they had been stripped of during the Swedish period. As a result of the autonomy granted to them by Russian czars, the administration of power in the Baltic provinces, popularly known as the Baltic special order, differed from that in the other provinces of Russia. The Baltic-German nobility and the Czarist Russia were in agreement over this. Decline set in in Tallinn and the town remained a backwater until a railway line was opened from St. Petersburg to Tallinn in 1870. This triggered Tallinn's development into an important industrial centre and port town. Industry was soon booming and as peasants moved in to provide the necessary labour, the population redoubled. The pace of development was such as had never been witnessed in Estonia before.

The National Movement

The society began to gradually change in Estonia in the 19th century - serfdom was abolished, schools developed and the Estonians' awareness of their identity began to grow. Musical and theatrical societies were set up, schools opened and newspapers founded. Interest mounted in folk lore collection, the national epic, Kalevipoeg, was published and, in 1869, the first all-Estonian song festival was held. Ideas which so far had had a foothold in only a few brighter heads, gradually spread and took a concrete form. If earlier on, educated Estonians had been assimilated into the mainstream of Baltic-German culture, then now they discovered the cultural and national identity of their own people, and ideas of autonomy and even independence began to cautiously gain ground. It was a time of a search for common roots, an identity which had been suppressed ever since the 13th century foreign conquest. It was a time of enlightenment and growth, which occurred a hundred years later in the Baltic provinces of Russia than in western Europe. The centre of this movement was Tartu, a seat of education since the Swedish period. But the national fervour spread also to Tallinn where the Germans had to relinquish political power in the municipal council in 1904. The stormy events of 1905 in Russia did not leave Estonia and Tallinn untouched – after a brief freer breath the Czar's punitive expeditions struck back, killing dozens of innocent people in a peaceful demonstration and meting out punishments from whipping to banishment in Siberia and execution by shooting without any investigation or court procedure. The Czar's power was toppled in the Russian Revolution of 1917, and Estonia won greater autonomy from the new democratic government. But when the Bolsheviks took over in St. Petersburg, the nation's leaders took advantage of the confusion and proclaimed Estonia an independent democratic republic on 24 February 1918. Although the country was almost immediately occupied by Germans - World War I was still going on – the idea of independence germinated and when the Germans withdrew in November, the people stood up to defend their land against a new Bolshevik invasion. On the first anniversary of the Manifesto of Independence, State Elder Konstantin Päts was able to declare that the country was free of all enemy forces. A treaty of peace signed with Bolshevik Russia on 2 February 1920 in Tartu not only ushered in a time a peace but also granted Estonia Russia's recognition of sovereignty of her territory for all time. Recognition by most western countries followed in 1921, and that same year Estonia was admitted into the League of Nations.

Short-lived Independence

But Estonia could enjoy her independence for only a little more than twenty years. The young country concentrated on building up her democratic institutions, elimination of war damages and building up the economy. As before, industry concentrated in Tallinn, the port gradually regained its importance and the city scene was thoroughly renewed. Tallinn developed into a modern European capital. For the city, it was the second period of prosperity after the 15th century Hanseatic period.

World War II and Soviet Occupation

Russia's recognition of Estonian independence, given for all time, lasted only for twenty years. On the basis of a secret protocol to the Hitler-Stalin Pact of 1939, which determined the parties' spheres of influence in Eastern Europe, Russia pressured Estonia into accepting Russian military bases in her territory and in June 1940 first occupied and then annexed the country, after installing a puppet government and parliament. Parallel to this, the Baltic Germans, many of them from families with centuries-long histories in the Baltic area, were resettled to Germany at Hitler's call. For Estonians, the Soviet occupation meant hundreds of people arrested and killed, and thousands taken away from their homes and deported to outlying parts of Russia. Few of them ever returned. During World War II Estonia was occupied by both German and Russian forces. For Tallinn, the worst day of the war, as indeed all its history, came on 9 March 1944 when the Soviet air force carried out an air raid of the city. Large areas of mostly wooden houses burnt down to the foundations, leaving more than 20,000 people homeless. Also many historical building were destroyed, including Niguliste (St. Nicholas's) church and the Estonia theatre. A ballet performance was in progress at the theatre when the alarm sounded, and the public ran to safety in their best clothes, the actors in their costumes, to witness the destruction of a symbol of national culture built on a public collection in the early 20th century. The city was rebuilt when the war ended, but for the Estonians 1945 did not mean the end of suffering. After the return of the Soviets in 1944 reprisals were renewed on an even wider scale than in 1940–41 – only those who managed to leave the country to find refuge in the west could be secure of their lives. Estonia remained for five decades occupied by the Soviets who established in the country their foreign ideology and began to carry out a policy of Russification.

Independence Restored

After about four years of what is known as the Singing Revolution, Estonia re-established her independence on 20 August 1991. Contrary to many other Soviet-occupied countries of Eastern Europe, Estonia managed to navigate clear of bloodshed as she moved from the status of a Soviet puppet "republic" to independence. But a large block of granite on Toompea still stands in memory of the tense days in August 1991 when the people barricaded access to the government and parliament seat there. They were prepared to fight for their long-desired freedom against Russian tanks.

Tallinn's Old Town

The Old Town of Tallinn consists of two parts, the Upper Town, or Toompea, and the Lower Town at its foot. If in the Middle Ages, Toompea was the seat of the bishops and the nobility, then the Lower Town was a free trading town in the Hanseatic League.

Toompea

All those wielding power in Estonia have done so from Toompea. It is the seat of the country's government and the parliament also today.

As historically, Toompea was the seat of the corporation of nobility, it was also where the landed gentry built their grand town houses. Most of them date from the period after 1684 when nearly all of Toompea burnt down in a major conflagration. The most noteworthy of Toompea's buildings is without a doubt **Toompea loss (Toompea Castle)**. First erected by the Sword Brethren in the 13th century, it was gradually built stronger until in the 18th century its east and south walls were torn down and rebuilt in baroque style to house the provincial administration. As a result of further reconstruction in the 1920s, the session hall of the **Estonian parliament,Riigikogu**, was built into the south wing of the castle keep.

Pikk Hermann (Tall Hermann)

The main corner tower of the Toompea Castle was erected in the 14th century and bears the traditional name given to main towers of German castles, Pikk Hermann (Tall Hermann). It is 46 metres high and is not just a symbol of the city but also the main flag pole of the country. After a fifty-year break, the Estonian national blue-black-and-white tricolour was again hoisted at its top in 1990. As the whole of the Old Town, also Toompea consists of two parts: the small fortress (castrum minor), or what we refer to as Toompea Castle today, and the big fortress (castrum maior), or the rest of Toompea. Although the small fortress has been rebuilt time and again, three of its original four corner towers still stand today – Pikk Hermann at the south-western corner, Pilsticker in the north-west and Landskrone in the north-east.

Orthodox Alexander Nevsky Cathedral

The Cathedral, erected during a period of Russification at the end of the 19th century, stands across the square from the Toompea Castle, a symbol of Russian power and Estonia's czarist past. Due to the circumstances of its building, it is not so much a valuable architectural monument as a symbol of an ideology. As most Estonians belong to the protestant Lutheran church so also most other churches in Tallinn are Lutheran, and the Orthodox cathedral with its onion domes is an exception from, as well as a contrast to the lofty spires of the Old Town's Gothic churches. The majority of these were already built in the 13th-14th centuries and constitute architectural monuments of real value.

Toomkirik (Cathedral of St. Mary the Virgin)

Toomkirik (13th-17th century) is the real pride of Toompea. It was supposedly built by order of the Bishop of Lund and dedicated to St. Mary the Virgin. Consecrated as a hall church in 1240, it was later rebuilt as a Gothic basilica. Its hewn limestone decorations suffered badly when the church burnt down in Toompea's great fire in 1684. Rebuilding started later in the same decade, and a baroque spire was added to the tower in the 18th century. Inside, Toomkirik leaves a plain and simple impression. On the one hand this plainness is typical of northern protestant churches, but is partly also due to damages of the 1684 fire.
Of the decorations, the most valuable is a collection of Baltic-German noblemen's epitaphs in the form of coats-of-arms.

Carved of wood, many of them by the renowned Tallinn wood-carver Christian Ackermann in the 17th century, these heraldic symbols are witnesses of Estonia's Baltic-German past. It is because the Cathedral was the Baltic nobility's parish church and also interments were carried out right in the church in earlier times, the right being reserved to persons of noble birth and the wealthiest of the town's merchants. Besides, the church features a number of grave monuments and grave slabs. One of the oldest monuments is to the Swedish army commander Pontus de la Gardie, in Renaissance style. Among other noteworthy monuments is one, in Gothic revival style, to the Russian Admiral and circumnavigator of the globe, Adam Johann von Krusenstern, a man of Baltic-German descent, of 1846, as well as to another Russian Admiral, the Scot Samuel Greigh, in early Classical style of 1788. Also the Cathedral's oaken baroque altar and pulpit are worth taking a closer look at. The Cathedral has an interesting bell cast in 1685. It bears an image of St. Mary the Virgin and the German text: "Come into the church at my ringing to prey and to sing praises. I was molten by the heat of fire and flew apart as the Cathedral unfortunately burnt down in the fire. One year later I was cast into this form and, as the picture shows, named St. Mary's bell."

A Walk around Toompea

Almost through a miracle a few houses on Toompea escaped destruction in the 1684 fire – those at 21 Toom-Kooli Street and 1 Rahukohtu Street. Both these houses date from the 17th century, while most other buildings on Toompea are of later origin. A well-guided tour in the citadel can turn into an educating trip through Baltic-German history. Directly opposite the Cathedral in Kiriku plats stands the former House of the Corporation of Nobility, where the Baltic-German noblemen from the province of Estland assembled for conventions. At present the building houses the Estonian Art Museum. But even more overwhelming than the individual houses is the atmosphere one feels walking along Toompea's narrow, winding streets. Several of them end at a platform from which open breathtaking views of the Lower Town down below, of the port, and the bay with two outlying islands, Naissaar and Aegna, guarding the passage into the Gulf of Finland beyond.

Short Leg or Long Leg?

Time flies unnoticed as you explore Toompea's charms. But before descending into the Lower Town you might want to have a snack or a cup of coffee. There are plenty of opportunities to do this, so why not choose a place in a historical setting. The Neitsitorn cafe in a former fortification tower directly opposite Niguliste (St. Nicholas') church and above the town's medieval armoury, or Marstall, has one of the best locations and also a fine view of the Lower Town opening from its wide glass front. In summer, you can sit in the walk along the top of the town wall. Entrance into the tower is through a passage in the town wall at the back of the Alexander Nevsky Cathedral. Before descending from Toompea, you must choose whether you do it by the Short Leg (Lühike jalg), walking down stairs through the Lühike jalg Gate with a massive iron-studded door and past artist Adamson-Eric's (1902-1968) house, now a museum, or by the Long Leg (Pikk jalg) running along the wall which once used to separate the two parts of Tallinn

All-linn, the Lower Town

At a call by the Order a large party of German merchants and craftsmen landed in Tallinn in 1230. They settled at Toompea's foot and built for themselves a church which they dedicated to St. Nicholas, the guardian of seafarers and traders.

Niguliste kirik (St. Nicholas' church)

The later Gothic Niguliste church (13th century) was the only one to have been almost completely destroyed in a Soviet air raid in 1944. Rebuilt after the war, it was no longer used as a church but turned into a museum and a concert hall. Today, Niguliste church offers not only the opportunity to attend to choral and organ recitals, but also to see valuable works of medieval art in as close a setting to their original locations as possible. The most renowned of the art treasures kept at Niguliste, which functions as a branch of the Estonian Art Museum, is a Danse macabre (Dance of Death) painting by the Lübeck artist Bernt Notke, as well as Niguliste's former main altar by another Lübeck painter, Hermen Rode, both from the 15th century.

As you emerge from Lühike jalg after descending from Toompea, you arrive at a street crossing immediately beside Niguliste church. Here you can decide whether you prefer to turn right into Rüütli (Knight) Street, left into Rataskaevu (Wheel well) Street or head straight on along Niguliste Street. If you feel like having a meal, you will find at least two good basement restaurants in Rüütli Street – Sub Monte and Mõõkkala (Swordfish). The latter, obviously, specialises in fish dishes. In the Middle Ages it must have given people the shivers to walk down Rüütli Street, for it was where the town executioner had his house. The executioner's sword, with the inscription, "God's mercy is new every day as I raise my sword to help a poor sinner into eternal life," can be seen on display at the Tallinn Town Museum.

A short way further on the street comes up to the town wall beneath the Kiek in de Kök cannon tower and, after a sharp left turn, emerges into Harju Street near the George Brown pub. Mainly blacksmiths and other craftsmen lived in Harju Street in the Middle Ages. Today, one of the sides of the street is empty – the street front there was totally demolished by Soviet bombs, so it is a monument, as it were, to the 1944 air raid. Rataskaevu Street leads past the Wheel Well, sunk in 1386, at the crossing of Rataskaevu and Dunkri Streets.

Raekoja plats (Town Hall Square), the heart of Tallinn

Traditionally, Town Hall Square represents the heart of the Old Town. It is where all the most important streets meet, a place where activity almost never stops. In the neighbourhood you will find some of the most fashionable shops in the Old Town. On a sunny day it is also a nice place to relax, sitting down in one of its outdoor cafes to have a mug of beer or a cup of coffee.

Raekoda (the Town Hall)

The most prominent building in the square is no doubt the venerable town hall, whose present Gothic appearance mainly dates from the 15th century, only the baroque spire being from 1781. At the top of the Town Hall spire stands one of Tallinn's best-known symbols – a weathervane in the shape of a medieval guard soldier, **Vana Toomas (Old Thomas)**, which has been standing there since 1530. Tallinn's Town Hall is one of the oldest surviving secular Gothic buildings in the whole Baltic area. A visit to the interior is strongly recommended, if possible, in connection with a concert in the tastefully restored Citizens' Hall. Be sure to see also the Council Hall with its its councillors benches with beautifully carved side posts (with scenes of David and Goliath, Samson and Delilah, etc.), carved friezes and lunette paintings. In the vestibule, the Town Hall exhibits pictures from the collection of the Brotherhood of Black Heads, but also the guest book with entries by numerous heads of state is interesting to see. Various temporary exhibitions are staged in the Town Hall's basement and the former Town Council's prison in Raekoja Street at the back of the Town Hall.

Chemist's Founded before Columbus's Discovery of America

The Town Hall is by far not the only noteworthy building lining Town Hall Square. One of them is the Old Town Council's chemist's shop, Raeapteek, one of the first of the kind in Northern Europe, founded in 1422 – long before Columbus's discovery of America – and has operated without a break to this day, with the exception of a recent closure for restoration. About 150 years after its establishment the shop was bought by Johann Burhardt, a man of Hungarian descent, and remained in the family until the 20th century. The selection of articles so much surpassed what can be had at a chemist's today. You could buy playing cards, tobacco, shooting powder, fruit wine and many other things. Of medicines, there was fish eye powder, lamb wool extract, black cat urine extract, dried frog legs and a lot of other mysterious tinctures and ointments. At any rate, Burchardts the chemists were so well known that one of them was even called to Peter I's death bed. The call came too late – news of the Czar's death reached the man before he arrived in the palace.

In Tallinn's history, the Burchardts are important also as owners of the first art collection in Tallinn, as well as founders of the first museum, Mon Faible (My weakness), in 1822. Town Hall Square itself has fulfilled a lot of different functions in the past – it has been the scene of gruesome executions and of merry festivals. It was also used to expose offenders in the pillory, for which purpose a neck ring with hand and foot rings is still hanging on the Town Hall facade. But the Hanseatic town had more reason to make merry. Wedding processions passed through the square, guests of the town were ceremoniously received there, carnivals were held and also a public Christmas tree was set up in it, for the first time so in the year 1441, according to records – earlier than in any other town in Europe.

The streets around Town Hall Square were lined with shops and craftsmen's workshops.

Also today Town Hall Square is the hub of various festivals and celebrations, above all at Christmas time and during the Old Town Days in early June. The everyday businesslike activity in the square is then replaced by animation and excitement as people flock into the Old Town to attend open-air concerts and theatrical performances, to browse among wares offered by medieval stalls, to watch blacksmiths demonstrating their skills and to listen to street musicians playing in the Old Town's streets. Folk dancers in their colourful costumes step up in the Old Town's little squares its and inner yards are turned into venues for puppet shows, open-air art shows or children's playgrounds. During one week it is possible to take part in hundreds of open-air activities for all tastes, free of charge!

Around Town Hall Square

From Town Hall Square streets lead to other interesting parts of the Old Town. The names of Kinga (Shoe) Street, Apteegi (Chemist's) Street and Kullassepa (Goldsmith) Street refer to the one-time specialisation of the streets' shops. Mündi (Coin) Street however, doesn't have anything to do with a mint, simmply one of the houses in the street once used to belong to a merchant and town councillor by the name of Mundt. A further interesting street is Saiakäik (White bread passage) which got its name after a bakery where a particularly good kind of white bread (Est. sai) was made, and its sweet smell filled the whole neighbourhood.

The Holy Spirit Church

At Saiakäik's exit into Pikk Street stands Pühavaimu kirik (Holy Spirit Church, 13th-15th century). The church, which initially served as a chapel of an almshouse, was later expanded and turned into the Town Council's chapel. In comparison with the Old Town's other churches, the Holy Spirit Church looks small and modest outside. But it has an interesting interior, and not just for its non-traditional ground plan – its has only two aisles, but its decorations, above all its famous Berndt Notke wing altar from the 15th century. Also the clock on the wall of the church facing Pikk Street deserves attention. Made at the end of the 17th century, it was the first public clock in town which shows the time of day also today. The Holy Spirit Church bell of 1433 is the oldest of all church bells in Estonia.

The church has played a significant role also in Estonian culture. In 1935, a Holy Ghost Church pastor published what is known as the oldest (partly) surviving book in Estonian – a catechism translated in co-operation with Simon Wanradt. A colleague of Koell's, Balthasar Russow, wrote a sixteenth-century Livonian Chronicle and taught reading and writing to young men from among the common people.

The Holy Ghost Church still functions as a protestant church, and now and then it has services also in English.

Pikk tänav (Street)

From Town Hall Square, Voorimehe, Kinga and Mündi Streets and Saiakäik lead into Pikk Street, once the main streets of the Old Town. The importance of the street for the Hanseatic city is easy to sea if we reflect that it was the shortest way from the marketplace to the port outside Suur Rannavärav, the Great Coast Gate. It is where all the guild houses stood and many wealthy merchants had their houses. Their triangular gables, such as of Kolm Õde, the Three Sisters (Pikk 70), remind us of the historical centre of Lübeck in northern Germany. It was because Lübeck was seen as the Mother of the Hanseatic League and a model for other Hanseatic towns to follow. Also the law by which Tallinn was ruled from the 13th to the late 19th century was adopted from Lübeck. If you launch on your walk down Pikk Street away from the centre, there's a nice place to have a cup of coffee at Maismokk (Sweet Tooth, Pikk 16), a cafe since 1864 with a pleasant late 19th century interior.

The Guild Houses

Directly opposite the Holy Ghost Street in Pikk Street stands the House of the Great Guild. As indicated by the date 1410 at the tip of the gable, the house was completed in 1410. The Great Guild was an association of the wealthiest merchants and shipowners, and only members of that guild could be elected town councillors of Tallinn. As a result, the Great Guild's coat of arms was identical with the small coat-of-arms of Tallinn – a white cross over a red field, and this coat-of-arms decorates the facade of the house also today. At present, it houses the Estonian History Museum in what is the town's biggest surviving Gothic hall.

Further down Pikk Street there are more guild houses. St. Canute's Guild which, besides merchants, had also craftsmen among its members, had its headquarters at 20 Pikk Street. The present eclectic facade of the house dates from the 1860s. Almost next door, at Pikk 24, is the house of St. Olaf's Guild, which enrolled also craftsmen of Estonian descent. St. Olaf's Guild members were not permitted to wear clothes of silk, velvet or taffeta, as this right was reserved only to merchants of German descent.

Entrance into St. Olaf's Guild, which has a beautiful vaulted Gothic hall, is through the neighbouring House of the Brotherhood of Black Heads. That house is remarkable for its well-preserved Renaissance facade, the only one from that period in Tallinn. The brotherhood was an organisation of young unmarried merchants of German descent and was so named after its black-skinned patron saint, St. Mauritius. The brotherhood's coat-of-arms with the black head of St. Mauritius can be seen over the front door. The hall of the building dates from 1908 when it was transformed from a former two-aisled hall with pillars down the middle. The Black Heads' portraits collection is on display in the Town Hall.

Kolm Õde (The Three Sisters)

On your way towards the harbour you will notice a picturesque group of three 15th century dwelling houses on your left (Pikk 71). A typical merchant's house in that period was laid out with only its narrow front gable fronting the street, while the rest of the building and all the outhouses extended into the interior of the block. The house had typically two rooms on the ground floor – a large front room known as the diele and behind it the sleeping quarters or the dornse, the only room heated by means of a hypocaust system from the basement. Deals were done in the diele and it also had a kitchen under a wide smoke hood in a far

corner. The floors above the diele and the dornse were used for the storage of goods (often grain) and had no windows, only goods hatches one above the other down the front. A beam for a pulley protruded from the top of the gable. The front porch was originally quite prominent, with special porch stones carved with the owner's coat-of-arms at its either side.

The ower's coat-of arms or initials can often be found also on pillar capitals and portals in the house. Later (in the 18th century) also the upper warehouse floors were taken into use as living quarters, and a large staircase with a gallery at the back was then built into the diele to provide access to the upstairs rooms. Well-preserved examples of medieval houses can be found in Lai Street (Nos 23, 29, 40) which runs parallel to Pikk Street, and also the Town Museum (17 Vene Street) has a diele which preserves a lot of its authenticity.

Oleviste (St. Olaf's) church

Oleviste church (first mentioned in 1267 but completed in its present shape in about 1500) stands with its facade towards Lai Street. Upon completion its spire reached to 159 metres and was thus one the tallest buildings in Europe. But in the course of history the church has been time and again struck by lightning (the worst disaster hit in 1625) and its present spire is only 124 metres high. According to a legend the church was named after his builder, a man by the name of Olev, but it is much more likely that the name derives from that of the Scandinavian saint, St. Olaf. The lofty nave and choir of St. Olaf's have beautiful star vaults and outside on the side facing Pikk Street there is rather an interesting cenotaph in a wall of St. Mary's chapel.

The Great Coast Gate and Fat Margaret

Passage out of the Old Town is through Suur Rannavärav (Great Coast Gate). In the Middle Ages, it was one of six gates the town had in its 2.35-kilometre town wall. Three fourths of the original 2.5 metre thick and up to 16 meters high wall around the Lower Town still stands today, and so do eighteen of the one-time 27 fortification towers. Next to the Great Coast Gate stands the powerful cannon-tower Paks Margareeta (Fat Margaret, 16th c.). It is 25 metres in diameter with walls more than four metres thick at the base. Today the tower houses the Estonian Seafaring Museum and on its flat ceiling is an observation platform with a good view of the port and the Bay of Tallinn, as well as a monument, the Broken Line, to the 852 victims of the Estonia ferry disaster of 28 September 1994, beneath the tower. Above the gateway on the side facing the port stands a beautifully carved small coat-of-arms of Tallinn. The date, 1529, marks the end of major restoration of the gate.

Kiek in de Kök

This is another of Tallinn's well-known cannon-towers which stands on Harju mägi (Harju Hill), a former Swedish-period bastion above Vabaduse Square. The Low German name of the 49-metrehigh tower means Look into the Kitchen – an actual possibility in the Middle Ages, considering the height of the tower and the design of chimneys in those times. The six balls from Ivan the Terrible's cannon were walled into the front of the tower in memory of the role it played in Tallinn's defences when it was besieged by Russians during the Livonian War. Today the tower is a branch of the Town Museum and serves as a venue for exhibitions and concerts.

The Dominican Monastery

Another branch of the Tallinn Town Museum is the Dominican Monastery at 12-20 Vene Street where a collection of medieval stone carvings from Tallinn is on display. The surviving parts of the 13th c. monastery which was never fully restored after its wreckage by mad crows during the Reformation in 1524, constitutes an authentic historical background to the open-air concerts and theatrical performances held in its secluded inner yard. The monastery's refectory was turned into a Gothic revival St. Peter's and St. Paul's church (consecrated 1845, the only Catholic church in Tallinn at present), but St. Catherine's church of the monastery itself (access between 14 and 16 Vene Street), is still awaiting restoration. Next to St. Catherine's, Katariina käik (St. Catherine's Passage), lined with small craft shops and

restaurants and with examples of Tallinn stone carvings exhibited on the church wall, leads into Müürivahe Street. Further down Vene Street stands the Orthodox St. Nicholas the Miracle-Worker's church, built in classical style in the 1820s.

Beyond the Old Town

The Old Town of Tallinn is surrounded by a belt of parks and tree-lined avenues. The parks, laid out when earthen bastions built in the Swedish period lost their importance in the 19th century, offer pleasant walks in the shade of age-old trees. Beyond the Old Town rise newer areas.

The main business district lies just outside the Viru Gate, between the Viru and Olympia Hotels. It is there you will find the biggest department stores: Kaubamaja, Stockmann, and City Sokos. Also the Estonia Opera and Ballet Theatre and Concert Hall, as well as the Drama Theatre are close by. The Linnahall concert venue which boasts of Tallinn's biggest amphitheatre (seating 4,800) lies on the coast next to the port. A new shopping and business precinct is rising in the area between Narva maantee and the port where old industrial premises are being adapted to new uses. Wooden suburbs from the late 19th and early 20th centuries form a semicircle round the Old Town. Kalamaja in the north is a comfortable walking distance away from the centre, and it is also the most compact of the wooden houses areas, where you feel like carried back a hundred years or so. Pelgulinn, Kassisaba, Uus Maailm and a few others lie a little further out. Bits of the old suburbs survive also behind the 1950s houses across Liivalaia

Street from Olympia Hotel. These rather rundown suburbs are now rapidly disappearing under the pressure of development. In the south, Nõmme, laid out in the late 19th century, is a green suburb with period villas and later private houses, and in the east, there are the green seaside suburbs of Pirita, Kose and Merivälja. But Tallinn also has its huge bedroom areas – blocks upon blocks of flats built of prefabricated reinforced concrete units in Mustamäe and Õismäe south-west and Lasnamäe east of the centre.

Kadriorg

The building of a baroque palace and the laying out of a park under the Lasnamäe cliff east of the town started in 1718. It was to be a summer residence for the Czar's family and was named Kathrintal (Est. Kadriorg, Catherine's Dale) after Czar Peter's wife, Yekaterina. The builder was Niccolò Michetti from Italy, and the complex was completed in 1723. After Peter's death, the palace was used to accommodate Russian rulers on their visits to Tallinn and was later handed over to the provincial administration. Before World War II it briefly served as a residence of the Estonian president and after the war became the seat of the Estonian Art Museum. This will be its function also after the current restoration of the building is completed. Forming the same complex with the Kadriorg Palace is an administrative building erected in the 1930s. Today, it serves as the residence of the Estonian president. The two houses are connected by a walled garden.

At a short distance from the presidential residence stands a small house under shady horse chestnut trees. It is the so-called Peter's Cottage, the house where Czar Peter I stopped during

his frequent visits to Tallinn while the palace was built. The house has been turned into a museum whose exhibits include Peter I's personal possessions. At the seashore in Kadriorg stands a monument to the Russian cruiser Rusalka which sank in the Gulf of Finland in 1893. The angel at the top of the monument points an Orthodox cross in the direction where the ship sank. The monument is by the outstanding Estonian sculptor Amandus Adamson (1855–1929) and was completed in 1902.

Song Festival Ground (Lauluväljak) and Pirita

From Kadriorg further towards Pirita along the seashore we come to the Song Festival Ground. It is an area designed to accommodate a public of about a quarter of a million with a huge choir shell to hold up to 30,000 singers at a time. This is the number of public and performers that turn up for all-Estonian song festivals every five years. Who has once witnessed such a large choir singing together to one baton will never forget the experience. The song festival tradition was laid in the national movement period in the 19th century, and the first all-Estonian festival took place in 1869. Nowadays, people arrive for the festivals from all parts in Estonia, wearing their colourful national costumes, which vary from parish to parish, so it is a feast for the eye as much as it is for the ear. Performers even arrive from Estonian communities abroad and the neighbouring countries. The programme features songs by children's, female, male and united choirs, as well as brass bands. Parallel to the song festivals, also folk dance festivals with thousands of participants take place in Tallinn, usually in the Kalev Stadium off Juhkentali Street. In the years of Soviet occupation the song festivals provided an opportunity for the Estonians to reconfirm to each other their will to preserve the

nation's cultural identity and to muster up strength to put up with the occupation for another five years. During the Singing Revolution in 1988 the Song Festival Ground served as an important venue for the people to get together and express views about their hopes for the future, both in flaming political speeches and songs. Also pop and rock music concerts, including by international stars, take place in the Song Festival Ground, and various other open-air events for large numbers of public are held.

Further east along the coast road you arrive at **Pirita**. On the shore at Pirita lies the Yachting Centre (Purjespordikeskus), a large complex built for the 1980 Olympic Games Yachting Regatta of which Tallinn was the host. Today the centre houses the yacht club and the Pirita Hotel, and the sports and fitness facilities of the complex are open to everybody, as indeed are its shopping centre and its restaurant. A picturesque view of the complex together with the sailing ships in the river mouth yachting harbour opens from the bridge over the Pirita. Across the river from the yachting centre stands Pirita's most important landmark, the high gable of the former Pirita convent's church. A convent of the monastic order of the Brigittines, whose mother house is in Vadstena, Sweden, was founded at Pirita in the early 1400s but was destroyed in 1577 by Russian troops laying siege to Tallinn in the Livonian War. On warm summer evenings, the ruins form a backdrop to open air performances and concerts, but a walk through the ruins and the surrounding graveyard can be very rewarding at any time of the day.

The Forest Cemetery (Metsakalmistu)

Further on, the coast road takes you to the Pirita beach and a beach restaurant (turn left into the pine woods about 700 meters from the bridge), and then to the garden suburb of Merivälja. But if you turn right at the first crossing after the ruin, it is a 3-kilometre drive to the Forest Cemetery (Metsakalmistu), a large graveyard laid out in an area of pine woods. There, on higher ground directly opposite a parking area are the graves of many prominent people – the poetess Lydia Koidula (1843-1866), the international chess grand master Paul Keres (1916-1975), the opera singer Georg Ots (1920–1975) and many others. Nearby rest the last remains of Estonia's first president Konstantin Päts (1874–1956), who died in captivity in Russia and was reburied there in 1990.

In another kilometre you will come to Tallinn's 1980-built 314-metre TV tower. 200 meters up the mast is a restaurant from where opens a wide view of the neighbourhood, with the Botanical Gardens directly below, and the nearby Baltic Sea islands clearly in sight. In good weather you can even see Finland from up there.

Rocca al Mare

At the other end of the town, on the coast of Kopli Bay, lies Rocca al Mare. It is the location of an open-air ethnographic museum, to which its foreign name was transferred from a summer residence of the industrialist Girard de Soucanton who had taken a fancy to Italy. The museum provides a good idea of how the Estonian peasantry lived in the 18th and the 19th centuries through authentic vernacular buildings transferred to the museum from all parts of the country. The exhibits are arranged into farmsteads and are furnished with original furniture, utensils and tools from the period. The museum also comprises a wooden church and a country inn. Folk lore groups perform at the museum at weekends. If you continue your drive further out of Tallinn from Rocca al Mare you will arrive in a fashionable summer resort area which stretches nearly all the way from Tallinn to Kloogarand, a very popular summer outing place for the people of Tallinn.

Nicolai von Glehn's House and Park.

If you happen to be driving in Nõmme, you can make a detour to von Glehn's House (48, Vana-Mustamäe Street) in the park off Tähetorni Street. The house, which bears a vague similarity

31

to Scottish tower houses, was built by Nicolai von Glehn (1841–1923) a man of Baltic-German descent, owner of the nearby Jälgimäe estate. Von Glehn is also responsible for the rise of the green suburb of Nõmme on lands which formerly were part his estate. By renting and then selling parcels of the land for people to build first summer cottages and then houses for year-round living he soon saw the idyllic summer place grow into a fast-developing community. Nõmme was granted the rights of an independent town in 1926 and was incorporated into Tallinn in 1940.

So we have had a brief overview of the most important sights in Tallinn, but would like to take this last opportunity to underline that these only serve as points of reference and you will find many, many more interesting things to see in Tallinn.

Text by Hanna Miller
English by Mart Aru
Photographs by Arne Ader, Mati Kose, Raivo Tiikmaa, Malev Toom, Toomas Tuul
Lay-out by Sirje Tooma
©HUMA.2001
ISBN 9985-898-04-4